The MEXICO Coloring Book

instagram: @jenracinecoloring

facebook.com/jenracinecoloring

www.jenracine.com

For COLORING

Put a piece of paper behind the page you are coloring if you are using markers.
It helps prevent bleed through and creasing on the next page.
Colored pencils, crayon or light markers are most suitable for this paper.

Use the internet to look up the sites in this book!
You can get ideas for colors and learn more about each place.

*Note: Information for states was found on wikipedia.com and other online resources. All information was believed current as of date of publication. Spanish language names were used except in circumstances where the English translation provides English speakers with greater understanding.

Find all JEN RACINE coloring books in online bookstores.

Find coloring pages on Etsy:
JenRacineColoring

Copyright © 2021 by Eclectic Esquire Media LLC
ISBN: 978-1-951728-68-7

No part of this publication may be reproduced, distributed or transmitted in any form or by any means, without the prior written permission of the publisher, except in the case of brief quotations embodied in critical reviews and certain other noncommercial uses permitted by copyright law.

About THIS book

Are you ready to explore MEXICO from Aguascalientes to Zacatecas?

This coloring book contains all 31 states plus Mexico City! Each is represented with capital city, flag, signature dish plus some distinguishing highlights such as monuments (like cathedrals), archaeological sites and UNESCO World Heritage Sites. Not every amazing site is included because there is not room on a single page to have all of the incredible places you can see in each state of Mexico. Enjoy your coloring journey through Mexico!

Did you know?

- Mexico has been a country since 1810. The name "Mexico" is believed to come from the Nahuatl word for "place of the Mexica."
- Mexico's official name is the "United Mexican States."

And...

- Mexico is 14th largest country in the world.
- Mexico has a total area of 758,450 square miles.
- Mexico has a population of approximately 125 million.
- Pre-Columbian Mexico traces its origins to 8,000 BC and is identified as one of six cradles of civilization.
- The Catholic Church played an important role in spreading Christianity and the Spanish language.

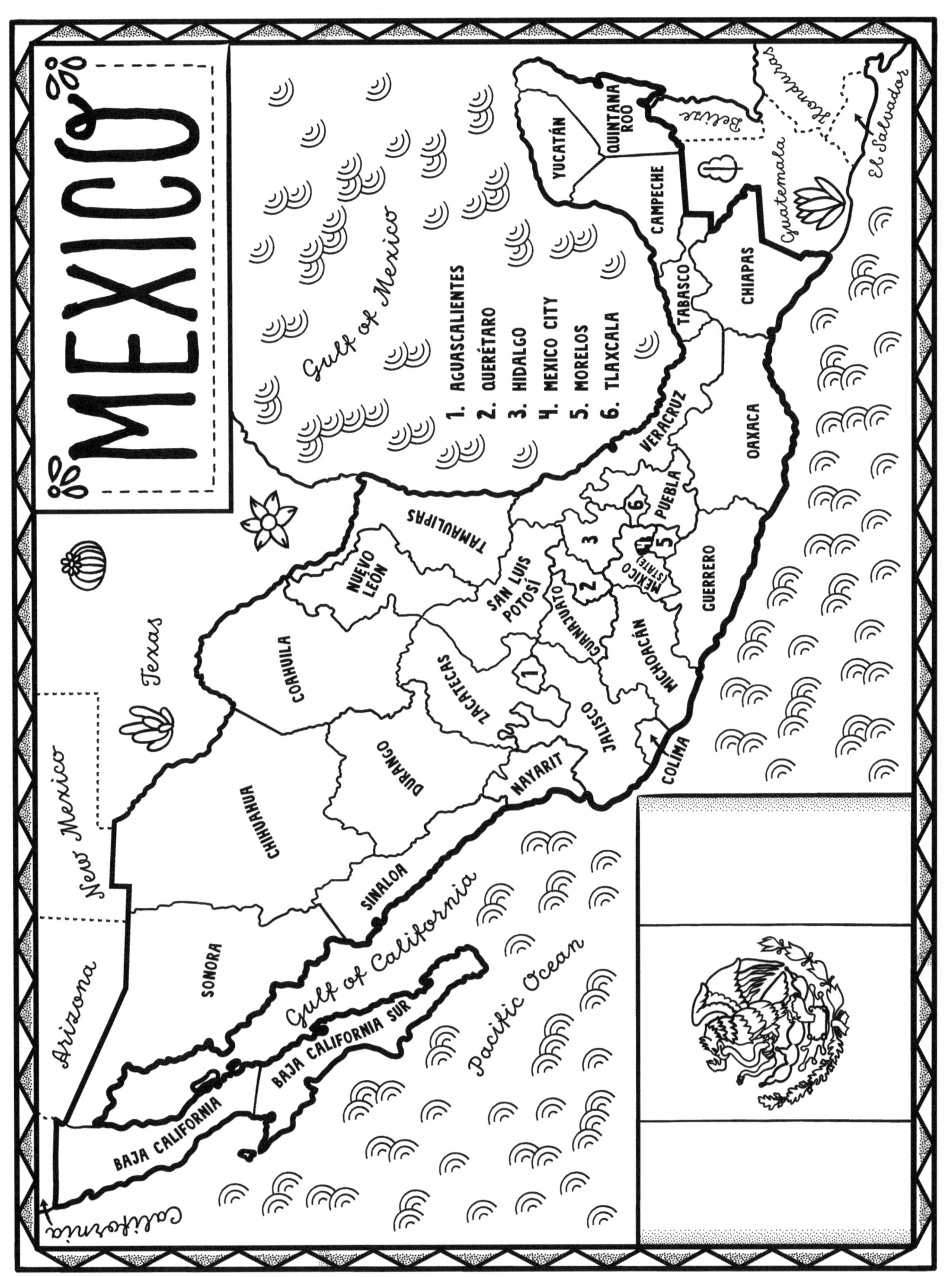

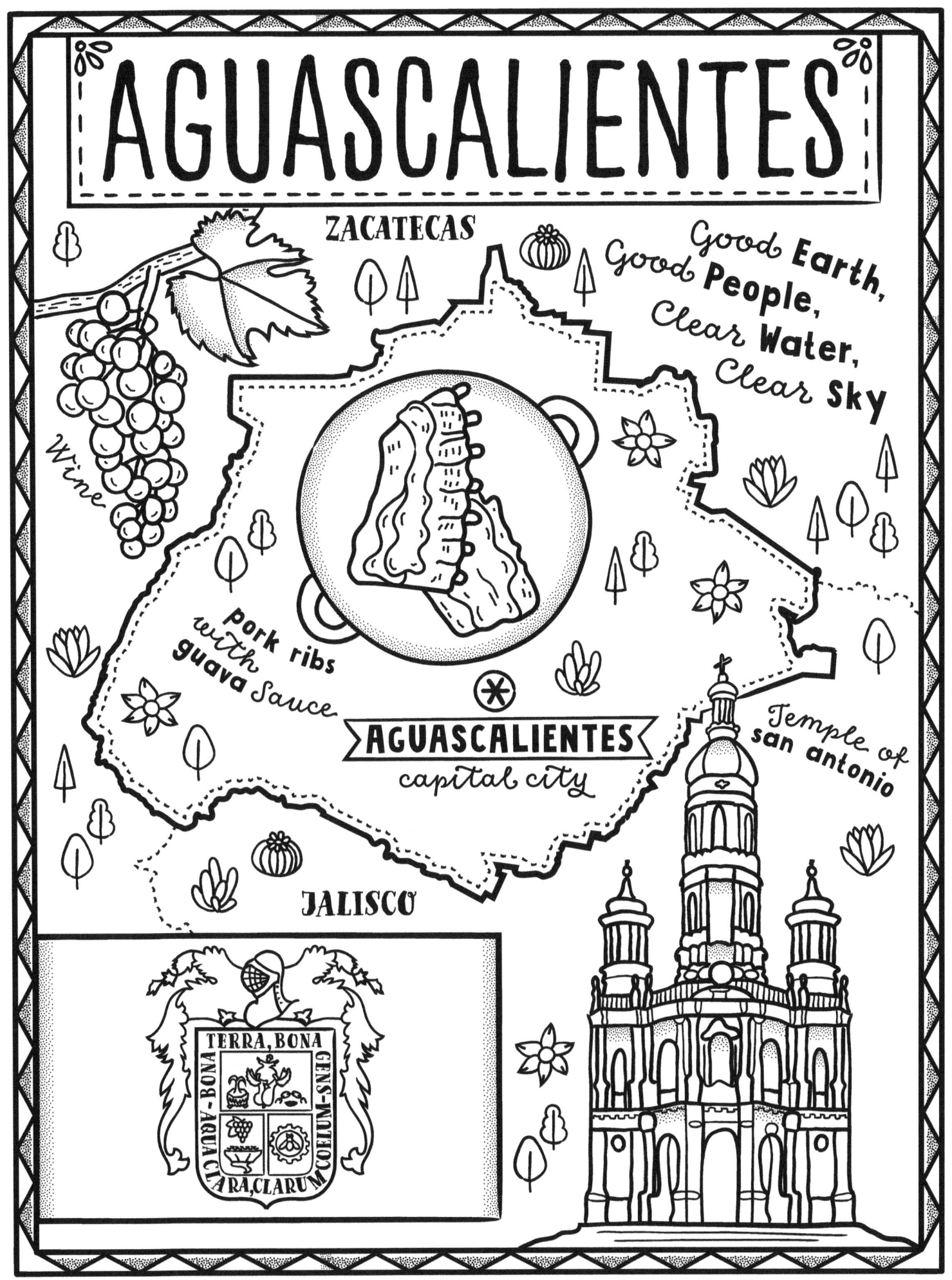

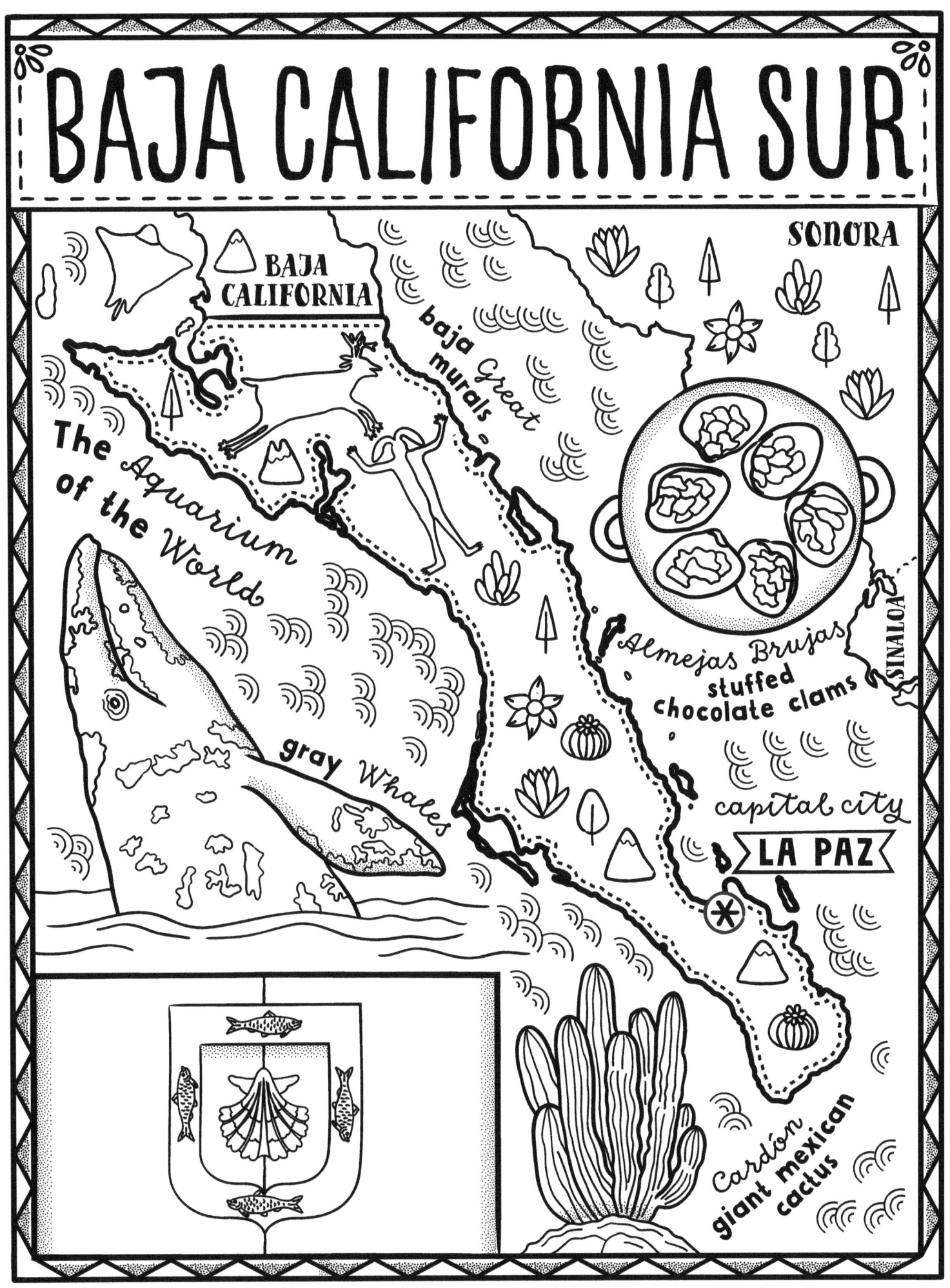

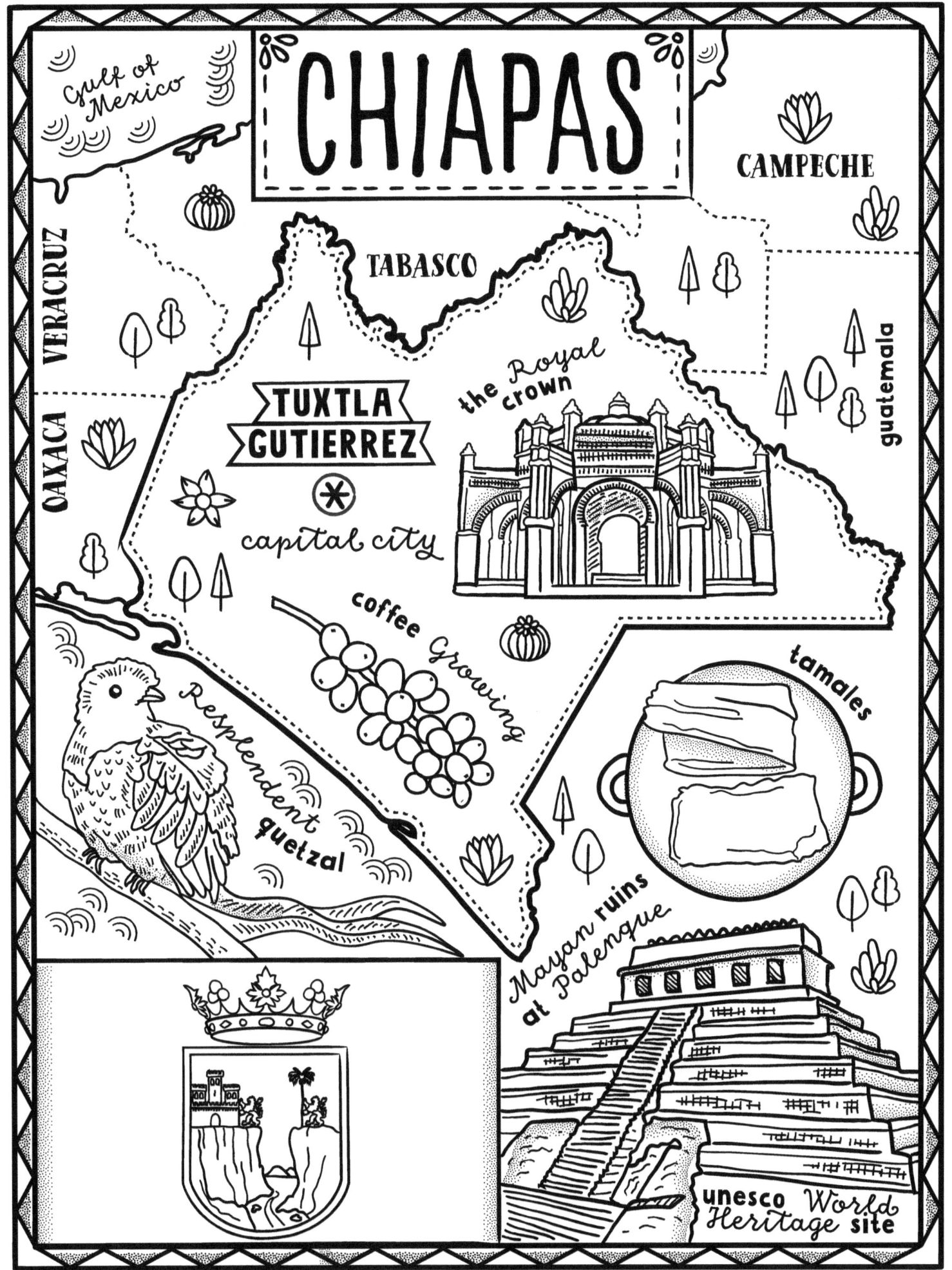

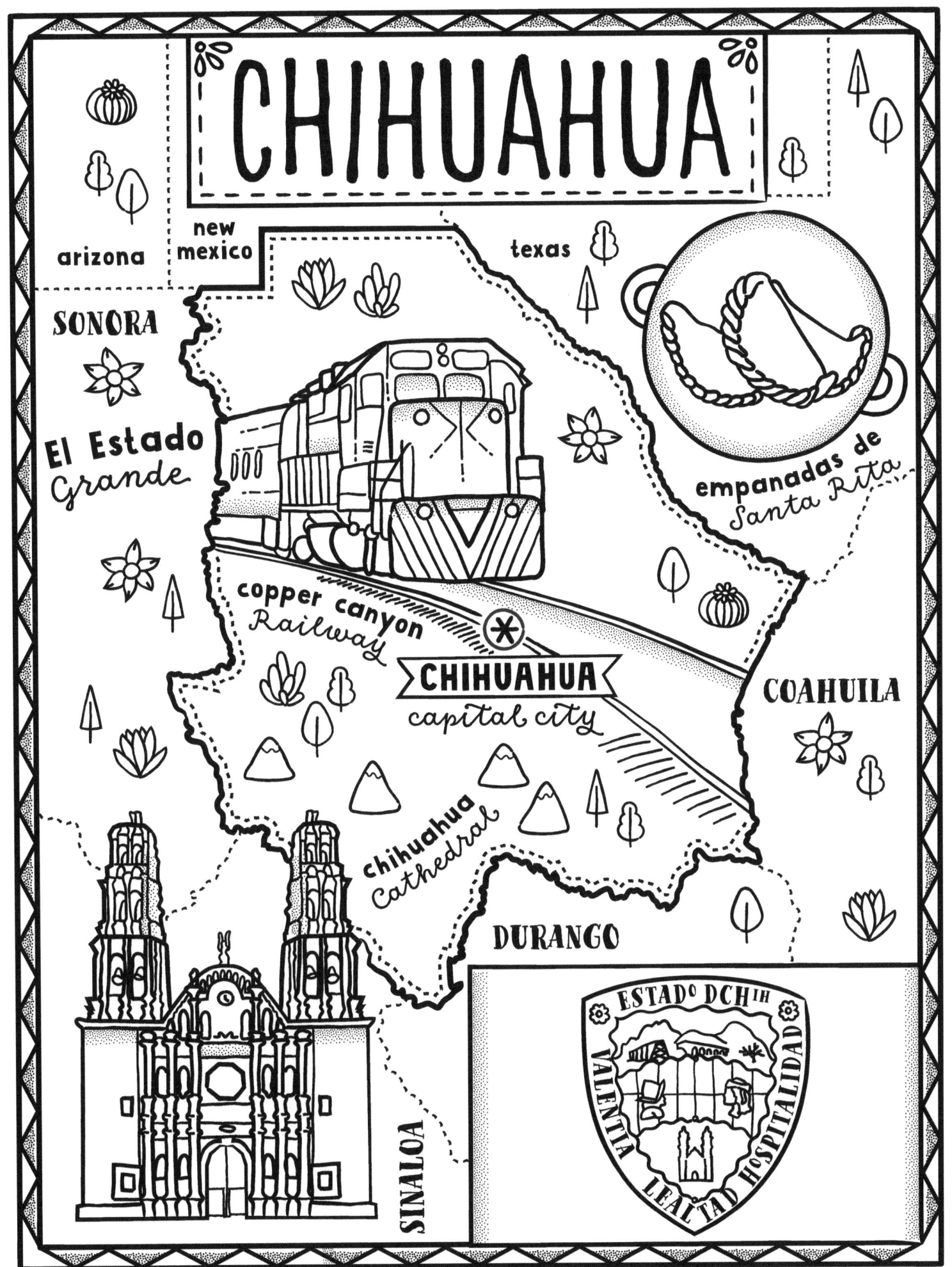

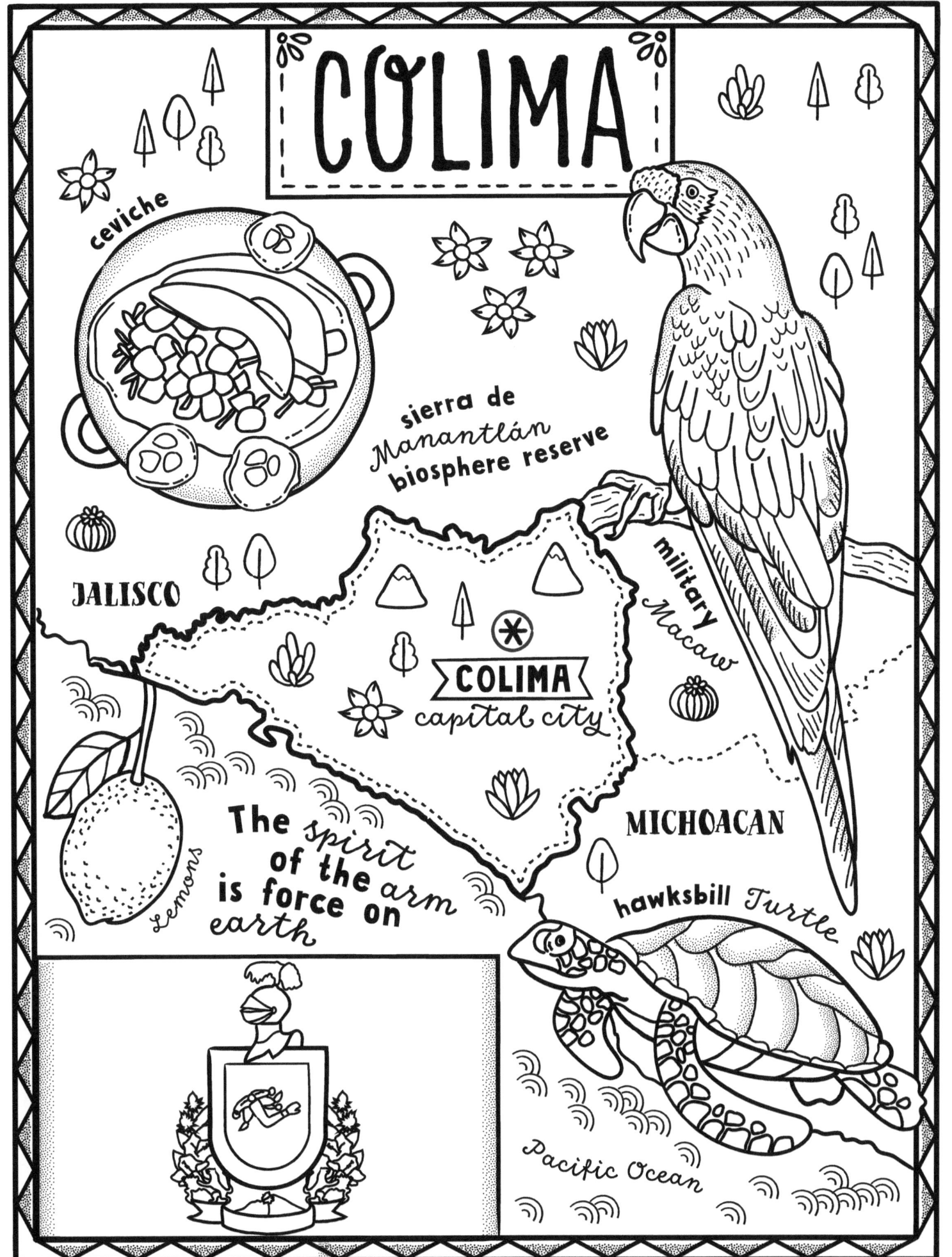

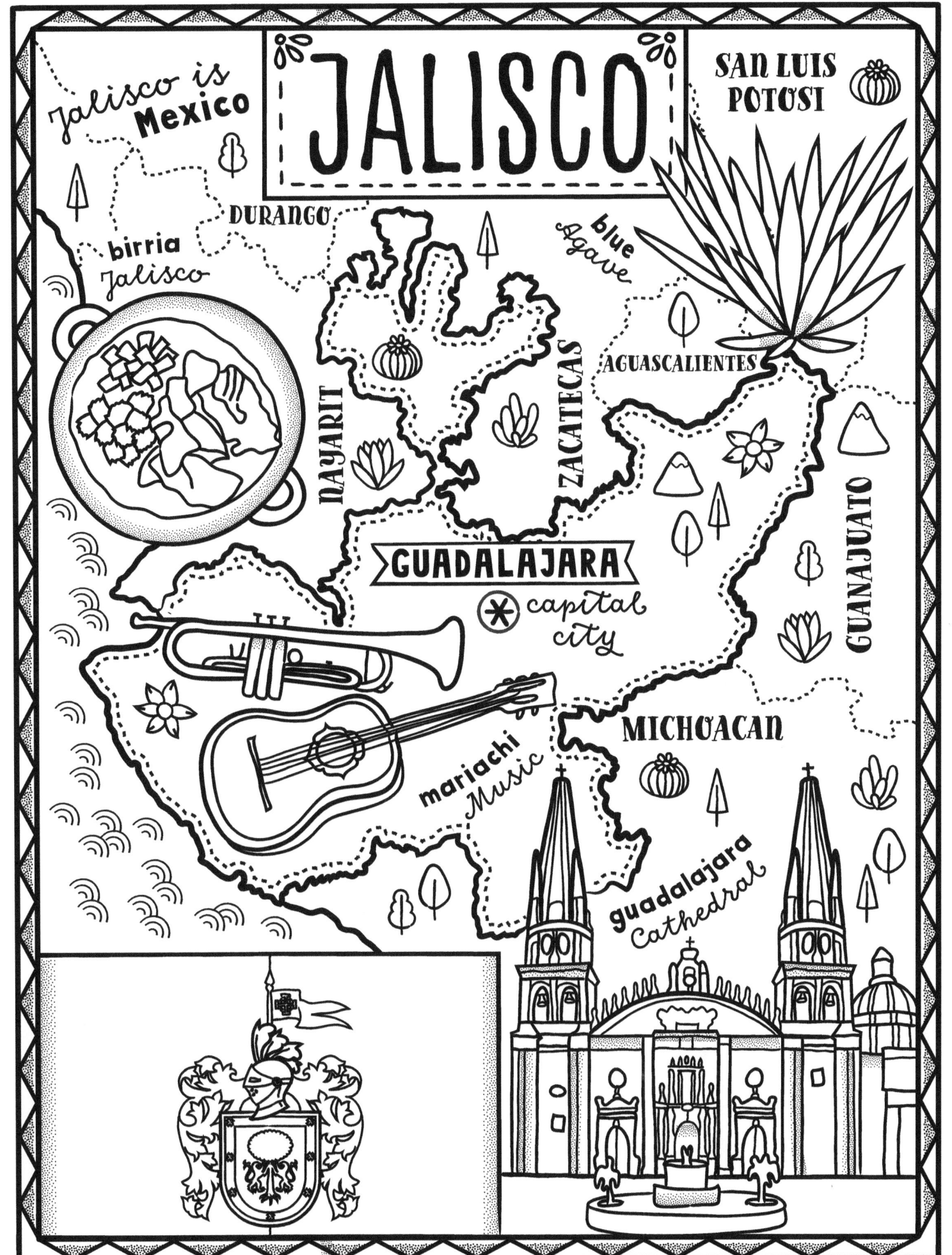

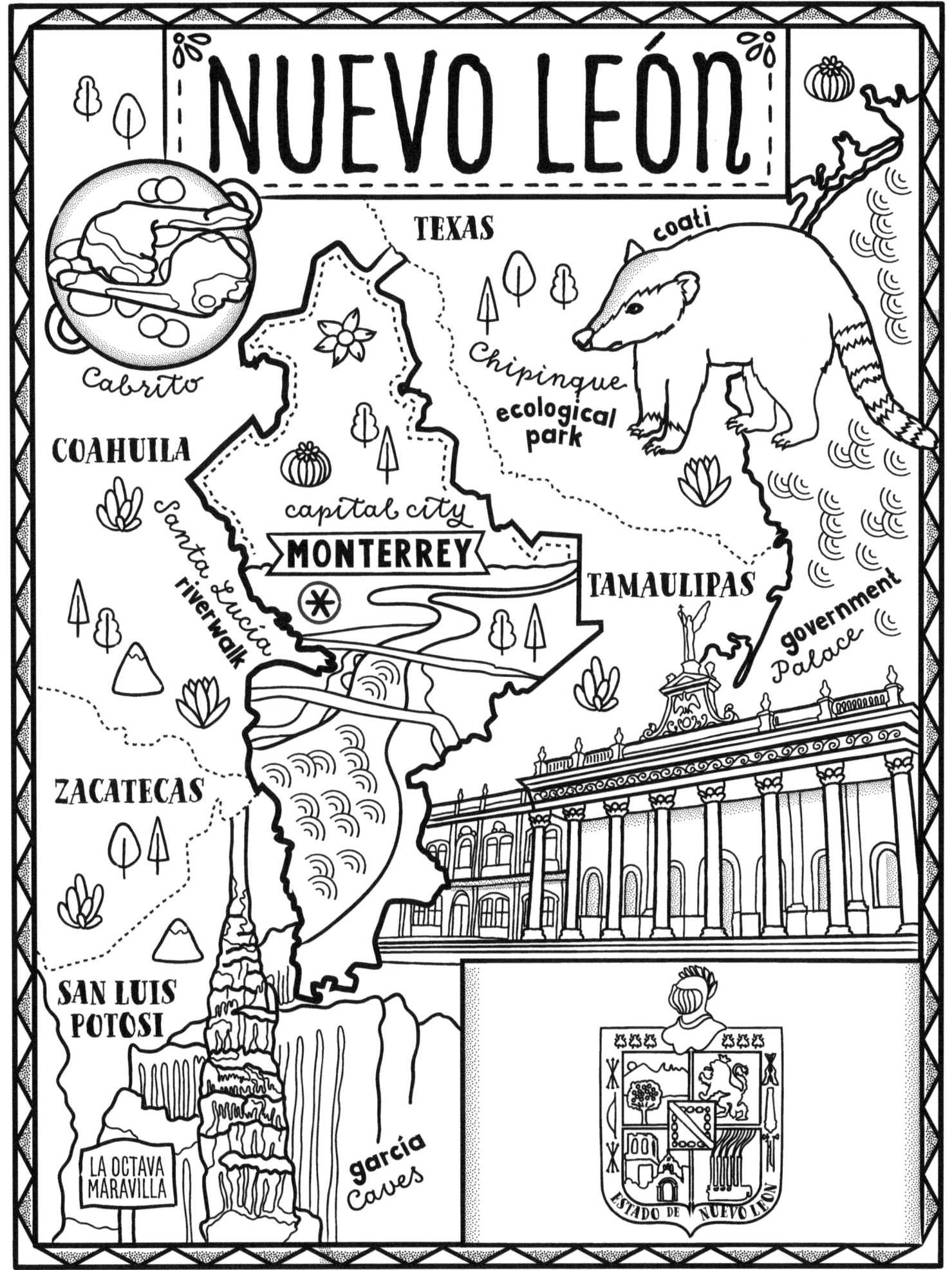

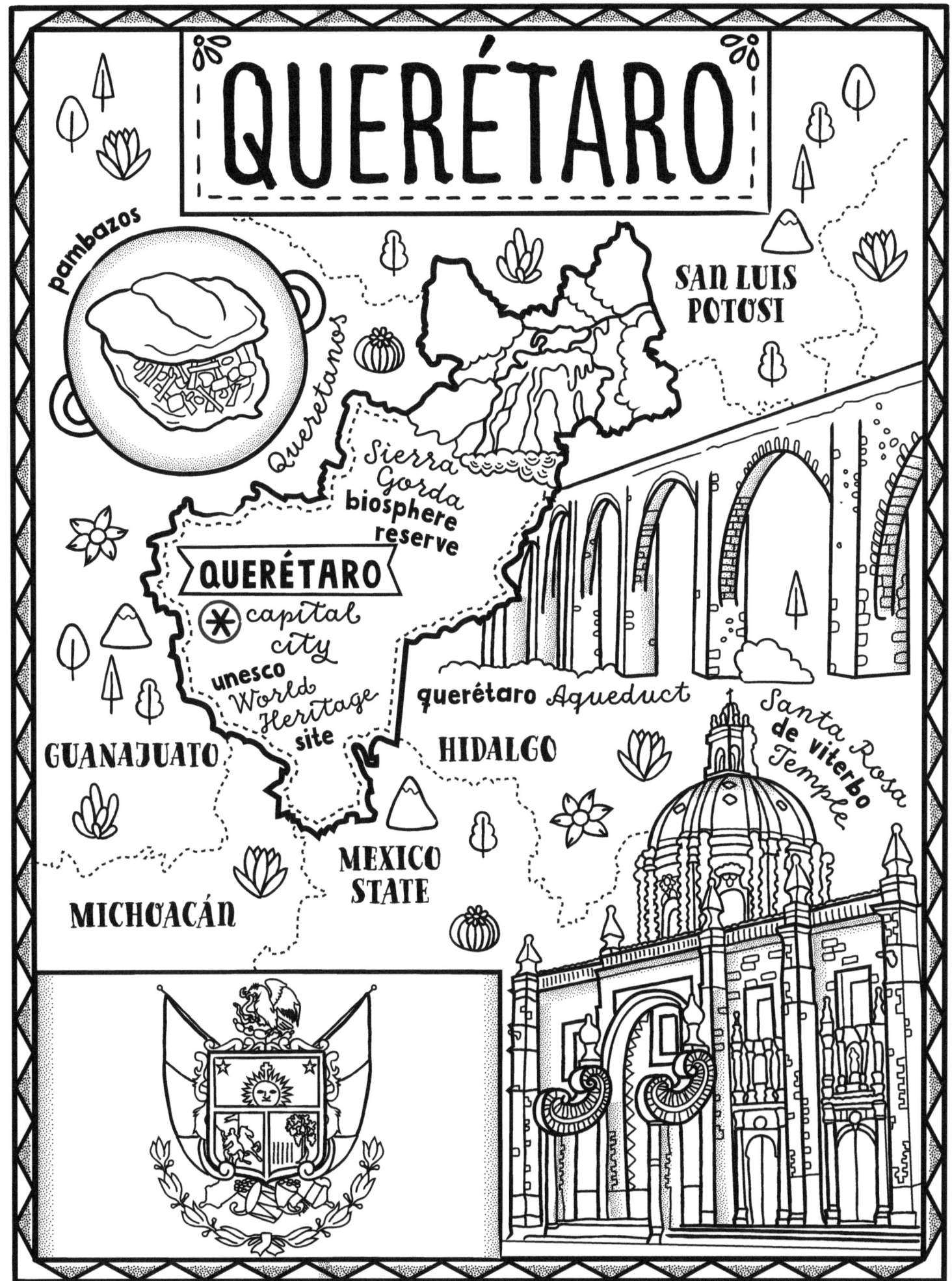

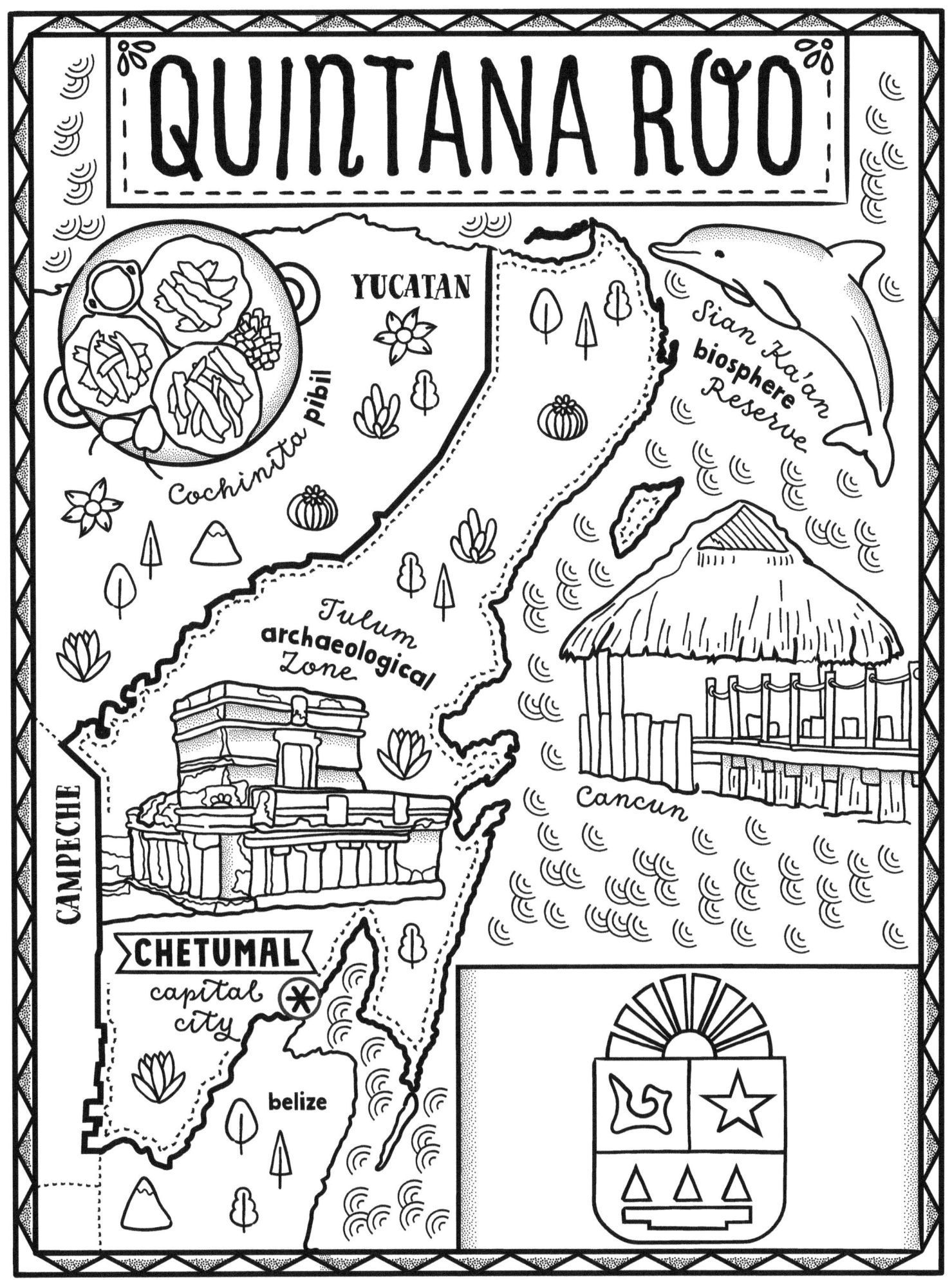

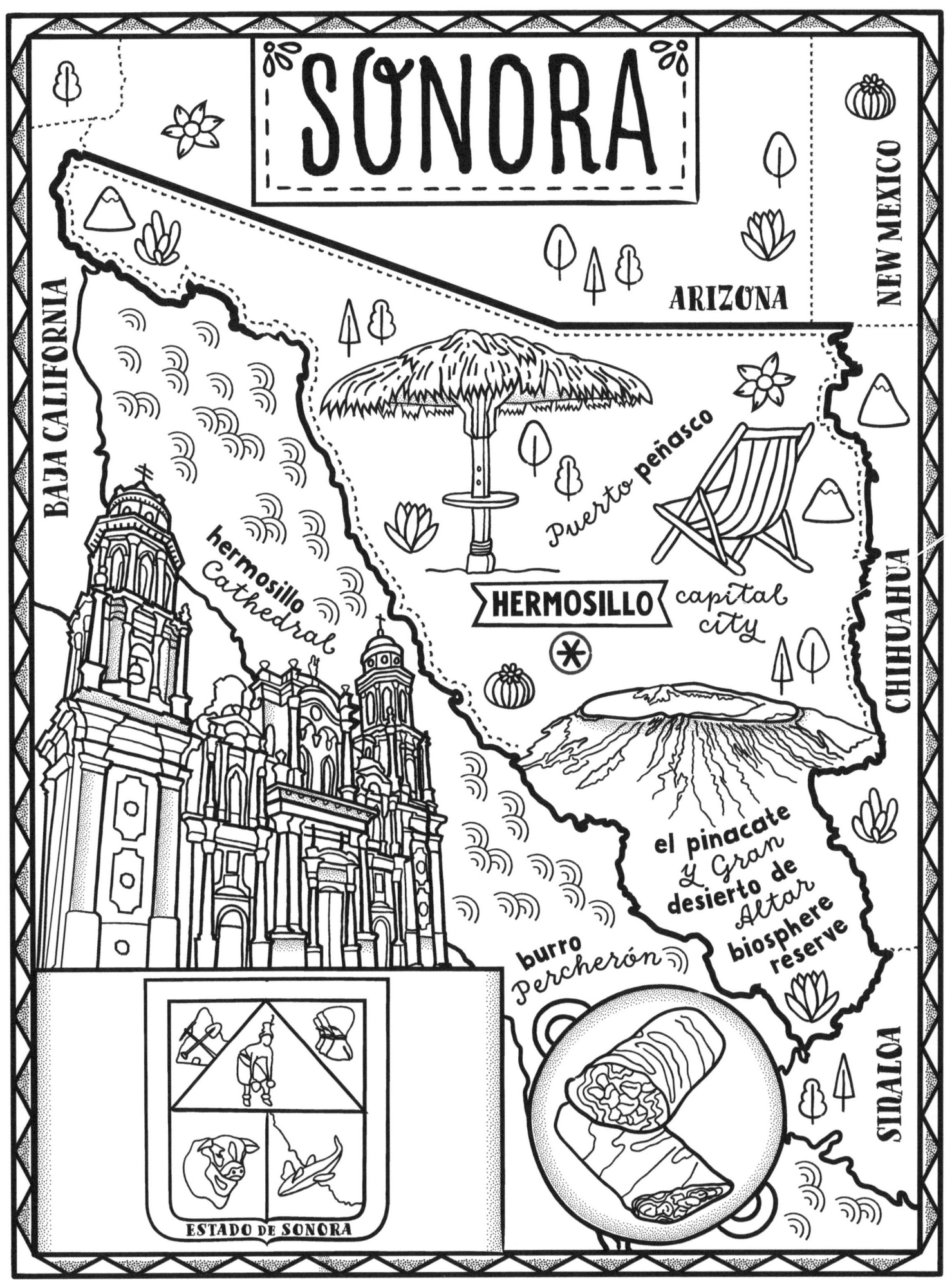

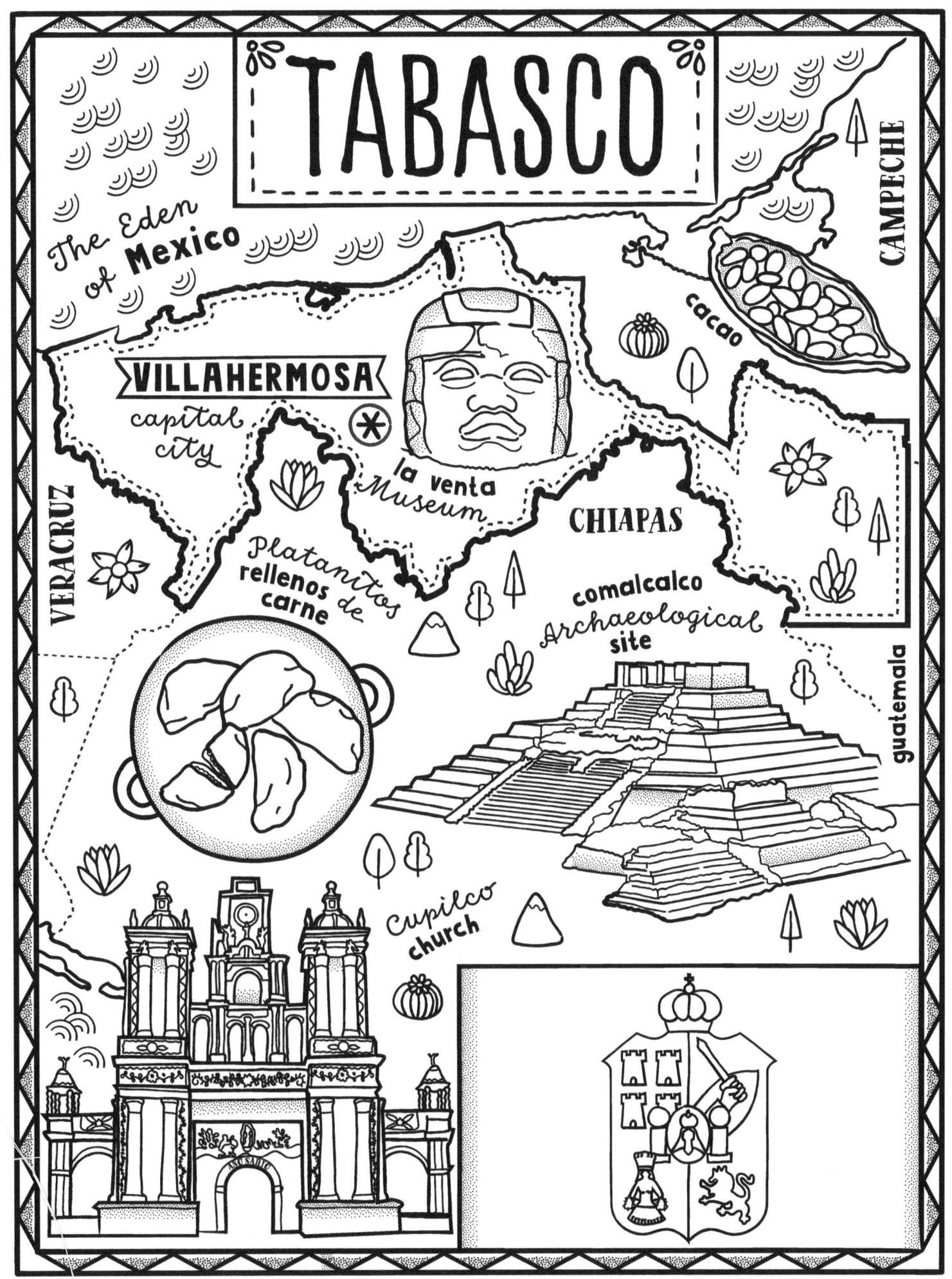

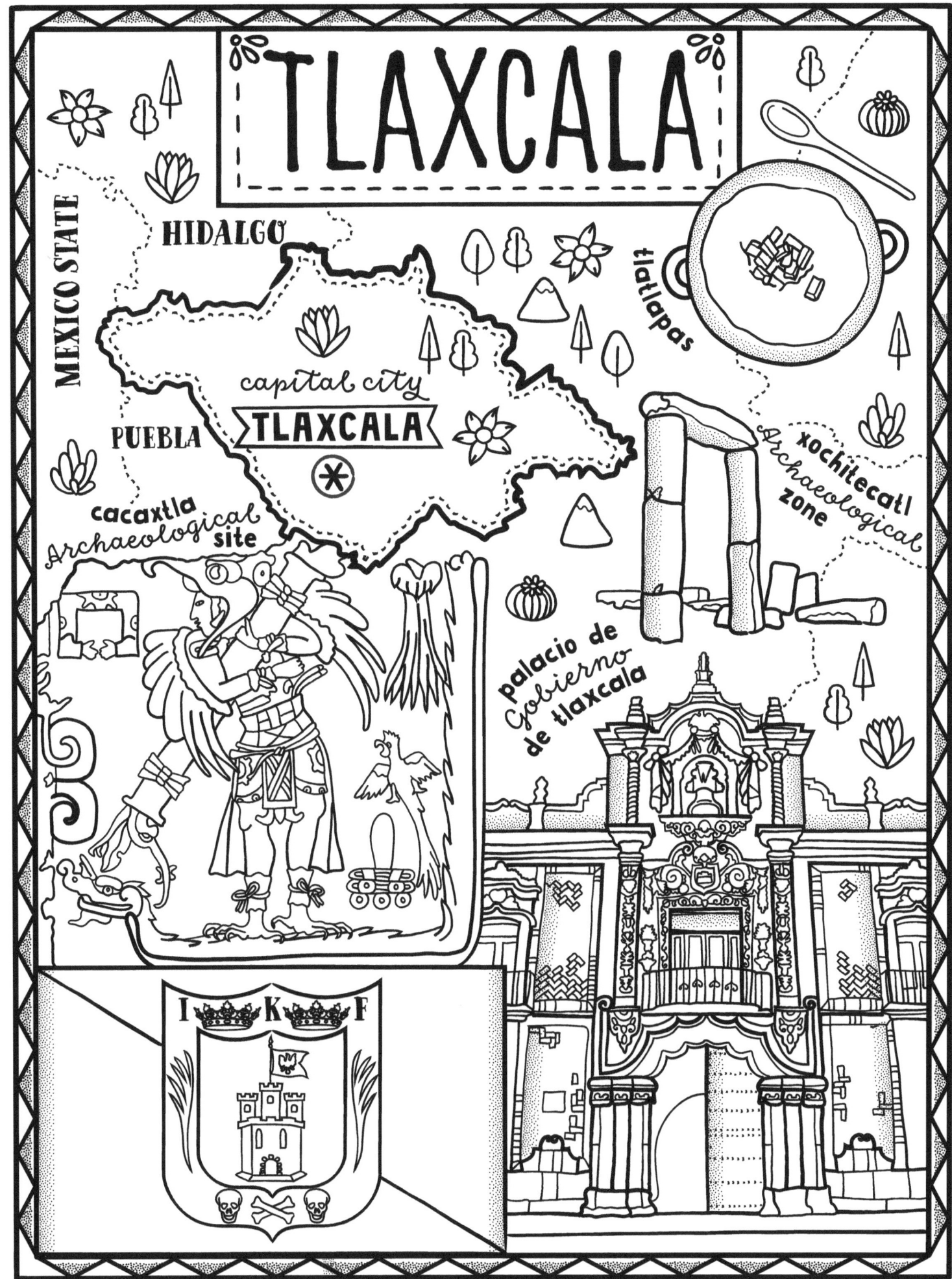

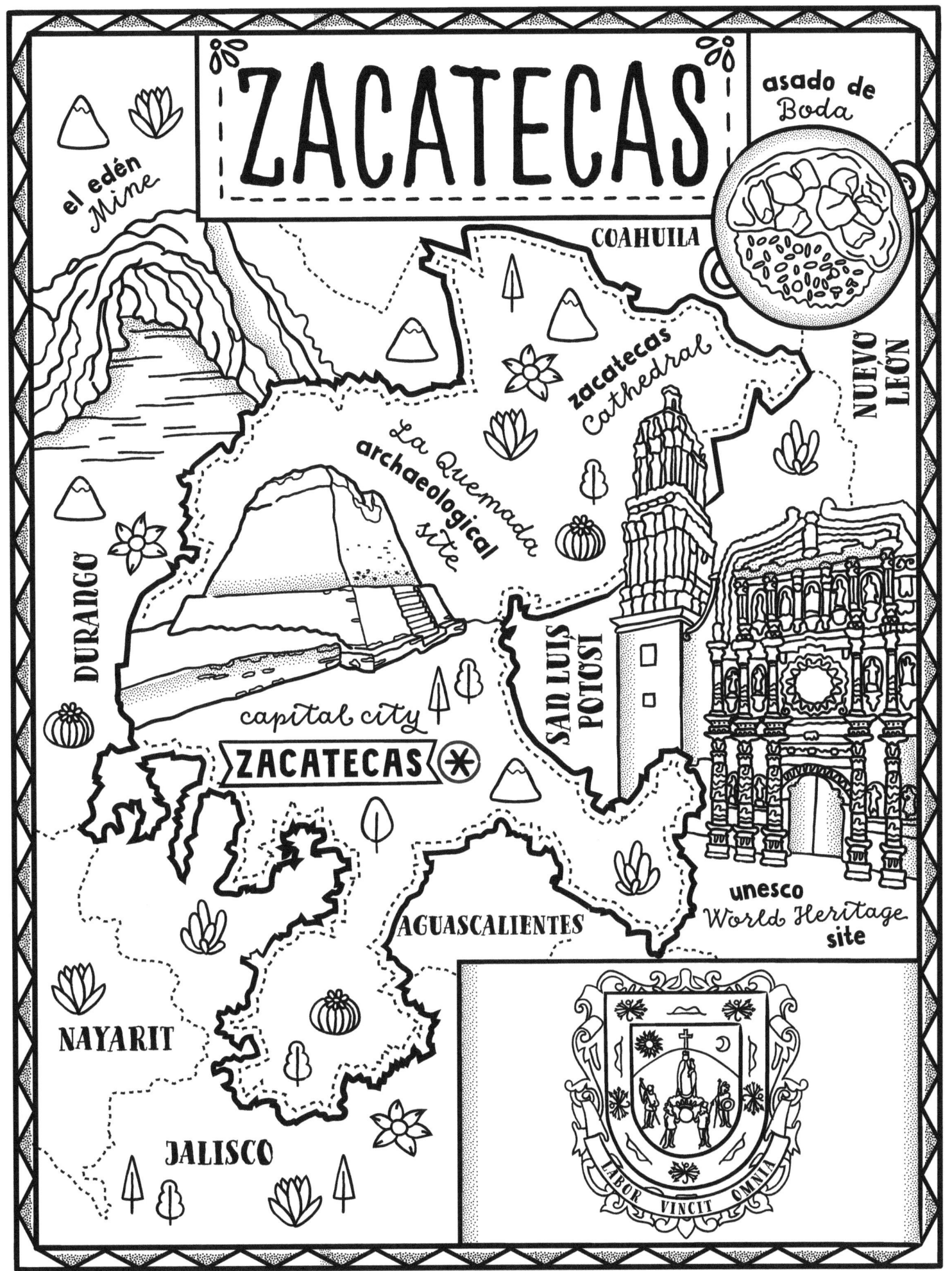